THE GREAT BOOK OF ANIMAL KNOWLEDGE

GIANT
ANTEATERS

Toothless Ant Predator

Introduction

Giant anteaters are the largest anteaters. They walk slowly on grasslands of South and Central America, using their nose to find anthills and termite mounds. Giant anteaters can attack an anthill and devour so many ants in only a minute! They are specially designed for this kind of lifestyle. Let's learn more about these ant-eating machines!

What Giant Anteaters Look Like

It's fair to say that the giant anteater is one of the more odd looking animals. They have a strange looking long snout, four legs, and a long shaggy tail. Anteaters may look strange, but they are actually designed very well for lifestyle.

Size and Weight

As their name suggests, the giant anteater is the largest species of anteater. They can grow up to 6 ft (2 m) long! And their long fur makes them look even bigger. Giant anteaters can weigh up to 140 pounds (60 kg).

Color

Giant anteaters are quite colorful. They are mainly colored either brown or grey. They have a black stripe that runs from under the snout, to their neck, and up their shoulders. There is also some white, light grey, or light brown surrounding this black stripe. The color of the giant anteater helps it camouflage from predators.

Tail

Giant anteaters use their large, bushy tails as a cover. When giant anteaters sleep, they curl up into a ball and cover themselves with their tail. Their tail can serve both as a blanket or a sunshade. Giant anteaters also use their large tails to help them stand on two feet only to fight off a predator.

Movement

Unlike other anteater species, giant anteaters only rarely climb trees. Giant anteaters walk around on all fours with their noses close to the ground. They usually walk at a slow pace. But sometimes they run with speeds up to 31 miles (50 km) an hour. Giant anteaters are also very good swimmers.

Where Giant Anteaters Live

Giant anteaters can be found in Central and South America. From the southern tip of Mexico all the way south to Uruguay. They live in grasslands, savannas, and rain forests.

What Giant Anteaters Eat

Can you guess what the giant anteater eats? Ants of course! Giant anteaters can eat as much as 30,000 ants a day! But they don't only eat ants; termites are also one of their main foods. They also eat grubs, bird eggs, and fruits, but these are not their main food source.

Senses

Photo by Kool Cats (flickr.com/katsrcool), as licensed under CC BY 2.0 Generic

Anteaters have poor eyesight. They find their food by using their nose. Anteaters have a very good sense of smell. Their sense of smell is said to be 40 times better than a human's sense of smell! Scientists are not exactly sure how good their sense of hearing is. Some say it is good while others say it's not the best.

Claws

Photo by Greg Goebel (flickr.com/37467370@N08), as licensed under CC BY-SA 2.0 Generic

Giant anteaters have strong claws on 3 of their 4 toes. These claws are perfect for digging into anthills and termite mounds. When the giant anteater walks, they curl their claws inwards and walk on their knuckles. This keeps the claws sharp and strong. Giant anteaters also use their dangerous paws to fend off predators.

Tongue

Giant anteaters have a very, very long tongue. Their tongues measure more than 2 ft (60 cm) long! There is sticky saliva on their tongues; this is what they use to catch ants. After digging into an anthill, giant anteaters can flick their sticky tongue inside 160 times a minute!

Protection

Have you ever tried to destroy an anthill and lick up the ants? Of course not! If you try this it will be very painful because the ants will bite you. Giant anteaters don't really mind these bites too much. They have rubbery skin and long hairs that protect them from these bites. However, they are not completely immune to ant bites, so they only feed for about a minute.

How Giant Anteaters Eat

After digging a hole into an anthill or termite mound, the giant anteater flicks its tongue inside to catch the insects. They only feed for about a minute at a time also because they don't want to finish the entire colony, they want there to be food available later. Giant anteaters don't have teeth, but they have stomach muscles that crush and grind the insects. They also swallow some pebbles which also help in digestion.

What Giant Anteaters Do

Ants and termites are not the most nutritious foods in the world. So the anteater has to conserve its energy by moving slowly. Anteaters also sleep a lot, they spend as much as 16 hours a day sleeping. When awake they spend most of their time searching for food.

Behavior

Photo by Michael Bentley (flickr.com/donhomer), as licensed under CC BY 2.0 Generic

Giant anteaters are solitary animals. This means that they live alone, except a mother and child giant anteater. Wild giant anteaters are diurnal, meaning that they are active during the day and rest during the night. However, it has been observed that giant anteaters living nearby humans are active during the night and rest during the day, nocturnal.

Territory

Giant anteaters are believed to be territorial animals. Each giant anteater has its own territory. These territories expand 1 square mile (2.5 sq km) each. Giant anteaters pee on their borders and stay away from others territories.

Breeding

Not much is really known about giant anteater breeding. It is believed that the mating season is during March to May. Male giant anteaters have sometimes been seen fighting one another. But still not much is really known.

Baby Giant Anteaters

Photo by Meg Rutherford (flickr.com/URL), as licensed under CC BY 2.0 Generic

Female giant anteaters are pregnant for 6 months. After this, they give birth to usually only one baby. Baby giant anteaters drink their mother's milk for about six months. They ride on their mother's back, camouflaged in her fur for safety. Giant anteaters stay with their mothers for about two years.

Predators

Photo by LaggedOnUser (flickr.com/47847725@N04), as licensed under CC BY-SA 2.0 Generic

The main predators of the giant anteater are jaguars and mountain lions. Giant anteaters try to escape these predators but if they can't, they fight back. Giant anteaters stand on their hind legs, supported by their tail, and slash at their predator with their claws. They can really hurt or even kill their predators! This makes them not a preferred meal for their predators.

Other Anteaters

Giant anteaters are part of the suborder Vermilingua (meaning worm tongue). There are three other anteaters in this suborder. They include the silky anteater, northern tamandua, and southern tamandua. They all look similar, they are all found in the Americas, and they all eat ants and termites. Other ant-eating animals such as aardvarks and spiny anteaters are not actually related to the giant anteater.

Vulnerable

Photo by CarolineL. (flickr.com/92208100@N03), as licensed under CC BY-SA 2.0 Generic

The giant anteater is listed as a vulnerable species, meaning that they are vulnerable to becoming endangered soon. Giant anteaters are sometimes killed for their fur or for sport. But the biggest threat to the giant anteater is habitat loss.

Get the next book in this series!

Polar Bears: Largest Land Predator on Earth

Log on to Facebook.com/GazelleCB for more info

Tip: Use the key-phrase "The Great Book of Animal Knowledge" when searching for books in this series.

For more information about our books, discounts and updates, please Like us on FaceBook!

Facebook.com/GazelleCB

Made in the USA
Las Vegas, NV
09 December 2024

13679723R00017